How to Train Your  Best Friend

20 Things Every Owner Should Do to Raise a Dog Right

Reyna Bradford

Flint Hills Publishing

How to Train Your Best Friend: 20 Things Every Owner
Should Do to Raise a Dog Right

Cover Design by Amy Albright

Flint Hills Publishing

www.flinthillspublishing.com

Printed in the U.S.A.

ISBN: 978-1-953583-13-0

Library of Congress Application Pending

Table of Contents

Foreword

P.H.A.R.M. Dog USA is a 501(c)(3) organization I started almost 15 years ago. PHARM stands for Pets Helping Agriculture in Rural Missouri. It was important to me to start this organization as a way to give back to all those farmers and ranchers that help feed us every day. Like any new organization, we needed support. I've met many people in life on this PHARM Dog journey, but one person made a lasting impression. That person was Reyna Bradford, the author of this informative book you're about to read.

After I connected with Reyna, I found myself looking forward to getting mail. Instead of advertisements and bills all the time, there was a consistent flow of cards and letters from her. She would share information with me about her dogs and what she was doing in her life with all of her animals. She would also send words of support and had interest in what we were doing to train our dogs to help farmers with disabilities. Those letters and cards came often and were always appreciated as our organization started to grow. Reyna wrote one last card that said I wouldn't be hearing from her very often, if at all for a while, but that she would always support us. She informed me that she was going to take some time away and concentrate on writing a book! She accomplished her goals when *In My Hands, Stories of the Animals I Love but Can't See*, was published in a couple of years later.

This second book that Reyna has written is full of helpful and informative tips with practical knowledge shared on how to train your "new best friend." Reyna's experience with training her dogs for AKC competitions, and everyday use of her dogs on her farm and in general, is invaluable information for anyone getting ready to start working with a new pup or even a refresher for people getting back into pet ownership. Training a dog to do something is hard enough as it is. Reyna has proven her dog training techniques work. And they work despite her having some extra challenges to overcome. This book is easy to understand and follow. It will be extremely beneficial to anyone that is learning to work with a new, four-legged buddy!

It was an honor to be asked to write this foreword. We're two different people, but we both train dogs and are both amazed at how intelligent dogs really are. Time and patience are key, and this book will help you to work toward accomplishing your goals of creating a long-lasting relationship with your new best friend.

Jackie Allenbrand
Founder & Executive Director of
P.H.A.R.M. Dog USA

Introduction

I have been living with blindness and with dogs for my entire life.

The blindness came first. I was just a toddler when a benign brain tumor left me with almost no vision. My left eye registers only dim shadows and basic contrasts. My right eye is completely without sight.

The dogs came soon after. I have loved dogs since before even remembered memory. They came initially as pets—playmates with soft fur, warm tongues, and happy hearts. Then they came as friends—loyal companions who guided me through many life transitions, including house moves and new schools.

More recently and better still, dogs have come to me as helpers and partners on my small but viable hobby farm.

I have always been fascinated by what dogs can learn, and how consistent training can benefit both themselves and their people. The histories and complexities of individual breeds have also captivated me.

For years, I have participated with multiple breeds in several types of canine competition. Obedience is my primary love, and I have trained dogs through the most advanced level of the sport. My dogs and I have also participated in rally, tricks, tracking, and barn hunt.

But besides the performance events, dogs have been invaluable to me at home. Raising registered Nubian dairy goats as I do, has made it necessary to gather multiple dogs of varying breeds around me. Many of these guys are working dogs with specific jobs to do.

There are large, livestock guardian dogs out in the pasture, protecting the goats twenty-four seven from any potential predators. And in the house, several capable stock dogs are always eager to dash out and round up goats whenever it's required. Added to that is the constant security of having so many eyes and ears watching out for me, in ways that I can't always watch out for myself.

Living on my own and running this place would be much more difficult without my dogs and their help.

Handling all of this without sight has given me a unique perspective on dog ownership and dog training. There is certainly no shortage of material available to anyone who wants to learn about raising a puppy, adopting a rescue, or training a dog for any kind of work or competition sport. Dogs are popular, especially these days, as more people stay at home with additional flexibility in their schedules. The "pandemic puppy" has become a global phenomenon. Everyone is scrolling the internet, swiping their smart phone, and leafing through books to find just exactly how to raise their new dogs right.

I don't pretend to have any inside knowledge or particular wisdom when it comes to doing dogs the right way. In fact, dogs are so popular that their proper care and appropriate training can often become highly controversial, flashpoint issues. I do not have all the answers. I don't know all the latest scientific research or the most touted training trends.

What I do have is practical knowledge and life experience. What I do know is how to be a competent leader to a group of dogs, even while lacking the significance of sight. It's not easy wrangling a household of nine or ten dogs, even when you can see what you're doing, never mind what they're doing, at any given time. But I have managed and I've managed while still continuing to enjoy them and succeed with many of them in the ring and on the farm.

My own positive, no-nonsense, effective approach is what I attempt to share in this book. It is not the only way to raise a dog right, and it may not even be the best way. But it does work. My hope is that it will work for you, and for your best friend.

Not everyone will agree with everything in the following chapters, and that's okay. You need to do what your own research and conscience dictate as best. The point is to ultimately give your best to your best friend, and I would love to help both of you along that road.

Tip 1
Pick the Personality, Not the Face

Dogs are cute. They look cute. They act cute. They give you those eyes. They give you those kisses. They have that soft fur and that stinky puppy breath.

Let's just be real here: People love dogs and dogs love people.

But when you're smack in the middle of a pile of squirming adorableness, or when you're walking past kennel after kennel at your local shelter, how should you honestly choose the dog that's the best match to be your new best friend?

For starters, do your research.

Go in with a basic idea of what you're wanting. Ask some questions of yourself and your family:

❀ Why do you really want a dog?

❀ What energy level can you handle?

❀ Is there a size you feel most comfortable with?

❀ What are you willing or able to put up with regarding grooming and shedding?

❀ Are there specific activities or tasks in which you hope to participate with a dog?

Be honest. Sometimes getting a dog does require some serious soul-searching.

It's easiest to do your research with a puppy, especially if you're acquiring one from a quality breeder. After all, if you've gone as far as picking a breeder, it means you've gone as far as picking a breed. Conscientious breeders will answer questions, tell you all about their specific breed (both the good and the bad), and will usually allow you to meet the puppy's parents, assuming that distance is not a major factor.

Many times, a good breeder will actually pick a puppy for you. This is done based on many factors regarding both you and the puppy. I was matched with my whippet, Banner, before he and I had ever met each other. His breeder knew what I was looking for in a puppy, assessed his litter for what most closely fit my criteria, and Banner came home with me several weeks later.

If you have a breeder willing and able to do that for you and your situation, then I applaud you, the breeder, and the puppy. You have shown that you care enough to share your hopes and requirements; the breeder has shown true concern for placing a puppy with the right person; and the puppy is entering your home with that kind of support. It's a win-win situation.

But what if you haven't worked with a breeder, and for whatever reason, are faced with making this life-changing decision on your own? What do you do when you're sitting in the middle of that puppy pile, or leaning over that baby gate, and you just have to choose?

Again, it should be the case that at least some research has gotten you this far. Please don't ever get a dog based on a snap decision or a sudden impulse. Bringing home a canine member of the family is an enormous commitment. For both your sake and the dog's, do not make it lightly.

But let's assume that you've thought this through, you've asked the tough questions, you know what you're wanting, and here you are back in that tumble of fur and cuteness, and you still have to answer that biggest of all questions: Which one do you take home?

The general consensus is to choose the middle-of-the-road puppy. Don't pick the one that's crawling all over you and biting the nose off your face, jumping on all its littermates and stealing everybody's toys. Don't choose the timid one that's hanging at the back of the group and hesitant to approach you. They both may be cute, but neither pushy nor shy is the ideal personality.

Ideally, you should pay attention to the puppy that is friendly, happy, plays well with the others, and is attentive to you. You don't want one that's incredibly mouthy, obnoxiously barky, starts squabbles, won't come to you, and doesn't want to be handled or held.

Because I do competition obedience with my dogs, I keep an eye out for puppies that are people-oriented and who take direction well. I want my dogs to be sociable, eager, and more on the submissive side.

But even if canine competition isn't your thing, here are some practical tests you can try to assess the personality of your potential puppy.

Pick up and hold the puppy. Handle feet, ears, tail, and mouth. Gently flip the puppy onto its back as you hold and interact with it. Of course, we're talking about a baby here, so there will probably be some wiggling, some grunting, and some mild chewing. But the puppy should not be panicky or defensive. You're looking for a baby that just wants to cuddle and be sociable and accepts what you do without a fuss. Remember to do your part with friendly, gentle interaction. Encourage the puppy to want to appreciate your affection.

When you set the puppy back down, watch the reaction. I like to see a puppy that turns around and solicits more attention from me. It's okay if the pup dashes off to play with someone else, but my preference is to see one that obviously enjoyed the time with me and asks for more.

What happens when there's a startling sound? If possible, have someone drop a metal bowl or something similar. It's fine for the puppy to act startled, but you're looking for a quick recovery time. You don't want to see any aggressive barking or charging, and you don't want to see any hiding or prolonged worry.

Check if the puppy will come back to you when you give the invitation. Again, remember this is a baby who doesn't know much. So be willing to get down on the floor and act silly. Use a higher-pitched "baby voice." Make kissy noises, whistle, clap your hands. If you can get the pup you're interested in to be interested in you and come to you, that's wonderful.

If possible, see how the puppy reacts when separated from the rest of the litter. It's fine if this results in some minor concern. After all, these guys have been together their entire lives. But as before, you don't want to see panic, obvious fear or frustration, or desperation to join the others. It's a very good sign if the puppy chooses instead to come to you and seek out your company.

Most puppies don't know how to walk on a leash or respond to commands. Most aren't house-trained or comfortable riding in a car. Those are your responsibilities to teach. They are not criteria as to whether or not you should bring this baby home.

It should also go without saying that puppies should be clean and healthy. By the time they're ready to be separated from mom and placed in homes, they should have had at least some of their immunization shots. Get the records from the person rehoming the puppies so you'll know how soon to follow up with your own vet.

Evaluating a dog adopted from a shelter, rescue group, or private individual can be harder. Dogs in a shelter setting especially can act very different than what they will in a typical home setting. No matter where you acquire an adult dog, ask as many questions as possible. Where does the dog come from? What is its history? How does it react to other dogs, cats, or children? Especially if you're adopting the dog from an individual who has owned it previously, get the details on why this person no longer feels that keeping the dog is a viable option.

The advantage of acquiring a pet from an individual person is that you can usually piece together most of the dog's history. You can also observe the dog in its familiar home environment, which will provide you a much more accurate impression of temperament and behavior.

Dogs who end up in a shelter program or rescue group will sometimes come with a known history, but many times will not. Reputable organizations will evaluate and screen dogs as stringently as they can before making one available for adoption. But again, bear in mind that behavior can radically change once a dog has been removed from the stress of kennel life (as experienced in a shelter) to the more relaxed comfort of a home. In other words, what you see or hear may not be what you actually get.

That can be a good thing, for example, in the case of a dog who acted very timid at the shelter, but who truly begins to blossom in a home. Or it can be a negative thing, let's say, if a seemingly calm and quiet dog in the shelter begins to act pushy and aggressive once a home territory and routine have been established. Rescue dogs do come with baggage. Some of it is inconsequential. Some of it is not.

That being said, there are definite advantages to welcoming an adult dog in to your family. Things like size and weight are already determined. House-training is easier. The chewing and general mischief of a puppy are largely a thing of the past. And an adult dog is ready to begin training immediately, if that's something you're planning to pursue.

Whichever avenue you choose to follow when it's time to bring your new friend home, the main thing to remember is to look deeper than just the cute face. There is, after all, so much more to dogs than meets the eye.

Tip 2

Exercise

This is something that I simply cannot stress enough. Dogs need exercise.

No matter the breed, no matter where you live, no matter the weather, no matter your work schedule, no matter how big your back yard might be, no matter how many other dogs you have. Let me say it again. Dogs need exercise.

If you're going to take on the commitment of sharing life with one, then you're going to need to extend that commitment to stepping up, stepping out, getting your rear in gear, and doing more than just a walk around the block.

I currently live with nine house dogs. The

majority of them are herding and hunting type breeds. They are high-energy, high-drive, and high-intelligence. They need roughly two hours of hard exercise every day. And that's what they get.

I think it's fairly well accepted that energetic breeds—border collies, Australian shepherds, Labradors, Weimaraners, and the like—do best with an exercise routine. After all, the logic seems to go, they are larger breeds with lots of energy. Therefore, they need to be walked.

But I'm going to take that logic several steps further and argue that all dogs need to be walked, regardless of breed, and that high-energy breeds in particular need much more than just a casual stroll.

I am fortunate enough to live on rural roads where my own canine crew can mostly run off leash. That is the ideal situation which many dogs don't get to consistently experience. If you do have the opportunity, there is nothing that can take the place of a long, off lead run for your dog. Dogs set free from the restraint of a leash can truly wear themselves out. They can also sniff and explore, both things that they love to do and need to do.

If, like me, you have multiple athletic dogs, walking them off leash gives them the chance to race, chase, jump, and even swim with the added fun of friendly competition. Besides the physical benefits, a pack of dogs that is walked and run together usually forges a more cohesive, stable group psychology. They leave the house, travel, and explore as a tight unit. They form a team. That's good for group bonding, and they learn to work with and understand each other better.

However, there is a major proviso to the off leash walking plan. It's absolutely imperative that dogs who are walked without the restriction of a leash have a solid and reliable recall. They must return to you when they're called. We'll talk about that in more depth later, but begin thinking about it now. You simply cannot unsnap that leash if you're not sure your dog will come back to you when necessary.

You also can't walk dogs this way if you aren't willing to be careful and considerate. Watch for cars and other possible hazards. Be a good neighbor. Be aware of people's property, livestock, and so on. It does take diligence. But if you and your dog can hit the country roads, there's nothing that quite compares.

Still, most dogs in modern society don't have the luxury of sallying forth into the big, wide world without a leash attached. For dogs who live in urban or suburban settings, your job as the responsible owner becomes a little more challenging. You still have to get that energizer bunny out for meaningful daily exercise, and you have to do it with the dog only three or four feet away from you and unable to run like a lunatic.

First of all, get moving. Walk fast. This is not sniffing time or potty time or catch-up-with-your-doggy-friends time. This is the time for brisk, forward motion, for both you and your canine companion.

I recommend no less than one hour of fast walking for just about any dog. Yes, that is an hour minimum, every day. Two or three hours is far better, but realistically speaking, many people just can't juggle that taxing of a time allotment with an already overcrowded schedule.

So you're out for about an hour. Make it count. Pay attention to your dog and to your own thoughts. Get your face out of your phone. Be aware of your dog and your surroundings. Enjoy yourself and the satisfaction of purposefully traveling with your best friend.

My opinion is that every breed and every size thrives on exercise. But once again, for the super athletic and energetic varieties, standard walking may just not be enough. That's especially true if those dogs live in a more suburban location where the leash can't come off. In that case, consider upping your speed and your dog's energy output. Consider long-distance running. Use a bicycle or rollerblades. One or two hours of that kind of speed will wear your dog out far more than the same amount of time would do at a slower pace. You don't just want your dog to be tired at the end of a day. You want him to be fulfilled. Breeds that were designed to run and work all day long desperately need an outlet to expend some of that energy, even in a city setting. If you have committed to bringing breeds like these into your life, don't let them down.

Another exercise option is a good, long game of fetch. If you have a dog who loves to retrieve, this can be a great strategy, and even better if used in addition to serious walking. It's especially helpful for urban dogs, since it does offer them a wonderful opportunity to flat out run for an extended period of time.

Even better than a routine ball game is to let your dog retrieve out of water. If your furkid loves the game, and if you have an accessible body of water nearby, water retrieval is a fabulous way to drain energy and fulfill the natural instinct to chase, swim, and bring back.

Of course, every so often the health or age of a dog, or the weather conditions you're handed on a certain day, may not allow you to do as much exercise as I've recommended. There are exceptions to every rule. Be smart about it, but also be intentional. Don't be lazy just because the weather is hot or cold or wet. Go half the distance so your dog can at least feel that he's been out, and can also see that this isn't the best day to be out in. Play a game of fetch instead. Work with what life throws at you. But don't be lazy. Don't let your dog down.

Remember the old saying: Tired dogs are happy dogs, and happy dogs make happy owners. The quote is not original to me, but I can't explain things any more succinctly. Give it a try. Your dog will love you for it. And with all the extra outdoor exercise, you might find yourself enjoying life a little more, too.

Tip 3

Socialization

Part of the joy of having dogs is the fun of sharing them with others. Whether that means participating in canine competitions, some cute tricks your dog can do, or just having a happy, well-behaved companion you can take out in public, sharing your dog's unique talent and charm with others is a rewarding experience.

It's also enjoyable for the dog. Just like us, dogs are social creatures. They need to interact, and they like to meet and greet. Basically, they enjoy being enjoyed.

But to make sure it is in fact as enjoyable as it should be, requires a lot of groundwork from you. Any dog that is going to get out and about and mingle with other people and other animals needs consistent socialization. Even dogs that don't get out much will still benefit from the variety and the confidence boost provided by social experiences outside the home.

The term "socialization" is just a fancy word that means exposing your dog to all kinds of new people, different places, and novel experiences. You want your dog to be stable, accepting, adaptable, and reliable in as many situations as possible. You also want him to live an enriched life, with horizons that stretch far beyond the backyard fence. In short, you want your dog to be social.

Socialization begins early in a puppy's life, and it continues throughout the years you and your dog will spend together. There is a lot of debate about what the right age is for beginning heavy socialization. Some opinions say the earlier the better, and others advise waiting until a puppy has had the full gamut of vaccinations before beginning outings. I tend to favor the first approach, but it's worth doing some personal research to determine what you think is best for your own puppy. There are pros and cons to both schools of thought.

Most puppies have experienced at least some minimal social interaction with new people before being placed in homes. Visitors come and go. Often times there are other pets in the household, which allows pups to get acquainted with additional dogs, and even with cats, pocket pets, and livestock. Most people, especially children, are eager to spend time playing with and handling young puppies.

So, you'll probably begin with a basic foundation already laid. Once you bring your baby home, it now becomes your task to continue building on it.

When you decide you're ready to begin going places, start with easy adventures. As an introduction to the larger world, I first start taking my puppies into pet supply and farm supply stores. These places are extremely pet-friendly and will gladly welcome your puppy. They both also have the advantage of wide aisles that are easy to navigate with an uncertain or boisterous baby in tow, and floors that are easily cleaned, just in case of accidents. Farm supply stores especially tend to be quiet environments, which is helpful for a puppy that might become overwhelmed by too much noise and activity.

However, both these venues do also offer experiences that a pup won't get at home. There are shopping carts and shiny floors. There are automatic doors, very unfamiliar smells, brand-new people, and even sometimes, brand-new dogs. It's a good way to get started.

Another thing that has paid off with my young dogs is to take them to our local biking trail. Not only does this offer the chance for them to meet new people and dogs, but they can also encounter odd spectacles like bicycles, skateboards, and baby strollers, not readily seen at home.

But don't just think about your dog's eyes. Remember that their ears, and especially their noses, are also dynamic ways in which they experience the world. Be aware of sounds, surfaces, and even smells that are new and different.

Take your dog everywhere you can. Go to parks, parades, and playgrounds. Attend festivals and high school sporting events. Go on longer car rides with your dog in mind and stop to walk and explore. Go downtown on a busy Friday night or a hectic Saturday morning.

Drop in at a local dog show if you can find one. This is a fantastic way to get your dog accustomed to many other dogs, applause, and lots of terrific dog people who usually have a few minutes to meet a puppy whose owners are really trying to do the right thing. You don't have to be an exhibitor to bring your dog into the crating and grooming areas.

I've even had success taking my socialization dogs to the entrance of Walmart and letting folks pet them as they go in or out. Check with the greeters at the doors and explain to them that you're training the dog and would like him to meet new people. Most employees will be happy to let you hang out for a few minutes.

Enrolling in a local puppy class or basic manners class can be extremely helpful. As a step beyond that, there are also programs offered through organizations like the American Kennel Club which can assist you in getting your new puppy or adult dog off to a good start. The STAR Puppy program and the Canine Good Citizen titles are just two examples.

The bottom line is that you want to expose your dog to as many new things as you possibly can. Remember that some dogs are a little more cautious than others, and some have already had good social experiences before coming to you, while others have not. The two of you will have a few negative experiences, but that's life. Learn to power through them. Most experiences will be decidedly positive. Always keep high-value, yummy treats with you, and use them generously.

Yet another benefit of intentional socialization is that you get to know your own dog better. So get out there. Learn about your dog, be creative, and have some fun together. Your best friend is definitely worth sharing.

Tip 4

Keeping Company

We've talked about the necessity of getting your dog out to experience new places and meet new people. Doing that is critical. But it's not the end of the socialization story.

Bringing people into your own home, and teaching your dog appropriate behavior when guests are present, is important, too.

There tend to be two extremes when it comes to dogs reacting to guests. One is a dog who is very territorial, barking, growling, and definitely not interested in friendly contact. The other is the dog who is frantic to meet and greet, jumping and pawing and demanding notice so that no one else can function and nothing else can be accomplished.

Most dogs are somewhere closer to the middle of the bell curve. But ideally, you once again want yours to be that stable, middle-of-the-road personality who greets guests politely and waits for further instructions.

I have found several strategies to be very helpful when it comes to training my own dogs how to best welcome visitors.

First is the "no touch, no talk, no eye contact" rule. When people come to your home, explain to them before they come inside that, for the first five minutes or so, they need to completely ignore the dog. This means exactly what it sounds like. Your guests need to be instructed not to pet the dog, not to talk to the dog, and not even to make eye contact with the dog, something that could solicit a reaction before the right time.

At first glance, this directive may seem a little harsh. People like interacting with dogs, particularly if it's a new puppy or a recent rescue. Sometimes your guests have even arrived specifically to meet the new addition. And now you're not even letting them say hello?

However, explaining that you want to begin training your dog right away, and that this is just part of the process, usually gets positive feedback. Assure your visitors that they're crucial to getting your dog's training off to a good start and thank them for being willing to help.

Everyone should remember that dogs learn about people first through their noses. Asking company to keep their hands to themselves for the first few minutes will encourage your dog to read and assess their scent before any further contact is attempted.

Finally, this is your house, your dog, and your rule. Visitors need to respect all of those things. Don't be afraid to gently but firmly insist on it.

Some people worry that by ignoring a dog they will somehow hurt the dog's feelings. Although this sentiment is well-meaning, it simply isn't true. It's treating the dog like a human. Dogs aren't emotionally devastated just because a new and unknown person doesn't fall and crawl all over them. In fact, as I just mentioned, offering a dog the chance to meet and greet first through the sense of smell is really much more respectful to the dog, since it's what they do naturally anyway.

It's an often-overlooked fact, but the truth of the matter is that dogs need to learn to be ignored.

It's not mean or thoughtless or rude. It is a critical canine life skill. Dogs cannot always be the center of attention. You have things to do. And, many times, so do your visitors. Repair people, remodelers, delivery drivers, etc., all come to your house with express purposes that do not include your furry friend. A dog that won't be quiet, or one that forces its way into the middle of everything without being invited, can be annoying, frustrating, and even a hazard depending on the job in question.

So, when you have visitors come over, even without the specific intention of meeting your puppy, the no-touch, no-talk, no-eye-contact rule lays the groundwork for a respectful, responsive, even-tempered dog who understands how to be patient and polite.

A second thing that I've insisted on with my dogs is the "all four on the floor" requirement. When it does come time for your guests to get acquainted with your dog, I recommend not allowing the dog to jump up. Once again, you're laying groundwork for the future. Jumping up may be cute in a ten-week-old puppy but think about it three years down the road. Especially with a large breed, or a high-energy type, those big, hyper front paws up on someone's shoulders may not be nearly as appreciated as a cute and harmless puppy hopping up on someone's knee. But it's the same behavior, albeit it miniature.

Consider who you're preparing your dog to meet. House guests aren't always going to be confined to close friends who love dogs as much as you do and who don't mind a little mud and slobber here and there. Be realistic. Someday it might be your elderly parents, or a coworker's toddler, or maybe someone who's afraid of dogs or who just doesn't appreciate them for whatever reason. You never know who will come into your house sometime down the road. Care enough about them, and about your dog, to prepare now for those future meetings.

I don't like my dogs to jump on visitors, and I don't like them to bark at visitors, either. For one thing, I have a lot of dogs. If they all started barking when someone came over, no one else would be able to communicate. But besides that, allowing your dog to continue barking at an invited guest is just rude. Even if the barking is friendly or excited, rather than aggressive, it still interferes with you welcoming your guest. It also allows your dog to take over your responsibility.

You are the owner of the house and the one who welcomes and converses with visitors. It's fine for a dog to announce that company has arrived, but your dog should know when enough is enough and when he's done his job.

Use a phrase like "that's enough" to let him know that you get it, that you appreciate him informing you, but that you've got it from here.

Some breeds are naturally more vocal than

others, and certainly this needs to be taken into consideration. But at some point, you should be able to ask your dog to be quiet and let you handle things.

One very effective method for a quick "quiet" is to take an empty pop can, drop twenty pennies into it, and then seal over the drinking slot so the pennies can't fly out again. Then, as soon as your dog starts mouthing off, shake the can hard five or six times. Most dogs will be surprised enough to stop barking and look back at you, and that's your opportunity to bring out the treats and praise and reward the quiet response.

Clashing two pot lids together also has the same effect. The idea is not to scare your dog, but to get his attention and stop the unwanted noise long enough to then offer a reward.

Think about actually teaching your dog a "greet" command. When it really is time for dog and visitor to meet each other, using a phrase like "go say hi" or "say hello" cues your dog that it's finally his turn to be on center stage.

41

Also, there's nothing wrong with encouraging company to dole out treats when the time is right. Especially with more timid or more territorial dogs, good food almost always builds good bridges. As the old saying goes: "The way to a dog's heart is through his stomach." You may have to keep some exceptional goodies around to hand off to your guest at the right moment.

And finally, what do you do with those visitors who are totally enamored of your furkid and adamantly claim that they love being jumped on and doggy-kissed and pawed over, no matter what you tell them? This is really your judgment call. Personally, I value my dogs' training and reliability too much to allow people like that to have ready access to them. I'm not going to let one person and their disrespect for my requests and rules to mess up months or even years of work. But if that's not an option for you—for instance, if the person in question is a close family friend or a nonimmediate family member who comes over often—then consider teaching your dog special permission for that one individual. Teach him that person's name. Or say something like "free time" or "go play." The bottom line is, give your dog specific permission to be rowdy with only specific people, if you have no other option.

Of course, there will be situations where dogs just aren't the best company for certain visitors. In those cases, use a crate—a strategy we'll explore in more depth later. Be mature and responsible enough to know when to respect both your guests and your dog, and just keep them separate. We know who's really missing out in those situations. Dogs are, after all, always the best company.

Tip 5

Make Vet Visits Positive

Although they are closely related to standard socialization, vet visits are so important and often so overlooked that they really deserve their own chapter.

Things are just different when you go to the vet. Many dogs who are normally stable and friendly become anxious or difficult as soon as they enter that fateful clinic door. And for some of them, the stress and panic begins much earlier. Some dogs just know when they're headed for a visit with a white coat. Whether it's the scents and scenery of the route you travel, the subtle cues that you yourself transmit, or perhaps just an inner knowing, a lot of dogs have figured out where they're going long before they get there. And a lot of them aren't thrilled at the prospect.

It can't be denied that they really have good reason to be stressed, or even frightened, at the doctor's office. Vet visits almost always involve pricks, pokes, proddings, and other liberties taken by a complete stranger. Add to that the plethora of odors—unpleasant chemicals, disinfectant, stressed animals, sick animals, and even stressed humans— and give your dog a little grace. The vet clinic is a scary place for many dogs.

However, you can take some big steps toward making these visits much more rewarding, and at least a little less concerning, for your dog. The unpleasantness may not go away, but your task is to attempt outweighing it with the good things that can and do happen.

A great place to start is just to bring your dog into the clinic for a simple meet and greet. Much like your excursions to pet-friendly storefront establishments, most of the time the reception staff at your vet clinic will be delighted to spend some time with a cute, new dog. If you feel that calling ahead to let them know you're coming would be helpful, they may be able to suggest a less busy time of day for the two of you to drop in. On the other hand, assuming there are no rules to the contrary, busy isn't necessarily bad. It will give your dog a nonthreatening sneak peek at the comings and goings of other people and animals in a typical clinic setting but will have no immediately negative associations for him.

Remember, though, that your main goal is to have him meet as many of the staff as you can. These should be viewed as future friends who will become at least semi-familiar and will be associated with positive interaction, before any unpleasant interaction is required.

Treats are always a plus. Use good ones. A strategy I have employed is to save the super high-value, incredibly yummy goodies for only those places where my dogs are likely to be the most stressed. Think cooked chicken, sliced deli meats, canned salmon, chopped liver, etc. Your treats of choice should be soft, easy to break, easy for the dog to chew, and with a definite smell that your dog can really appreciate. Divide them into small pieces so that less ends up being more.

Give some to the staff and let them "spoil" your furkid for a few minutes. Vets are busy, but if you can snag yours for a second or two and have him also become a treat machine, so much the better. Holding, snuggling, and sitting on the floor with your dog is also definitely to be encouraged with whichever of the staff is willing and able.

This strategy is most easily accomplished with a puppy, who thus far has no negative perception of the vet clinic. If you have an older dog who has been-there, done-that a few times already, success may not be quite as simple.

In this case, begin with a low-key waiting room visit. Duck in and let the staff know what you're doing before you even bring your dog through the door. Once you've explained things, go back to the car and bring in your dog without fanfare. Pick a quiet corner where you can both chill, and just sit for five or ten minutes. Again, don't forget those high-value treats. This time, it's you who gets to dole them out. Throughout the time that you've allotted for your hang-out session, methodically feed them to your dog, along with cheerful, gentle praise.

This approach is also helpful for timid puppies who are not as eager to meet the staff, or even for comfortable dogs who aren't necessarily anxious about the vet clinic at all. In either case, it's just a good thing to do. You want to convince your dog that this is a good place to be, and for those who already think it is, you want to remind them of it and reinforce that positive perception.

Once you've sat there about ten minutes, simply get up and leave. You don't need the staff to interact with your dog at all, and you don't need to go into any exam rooms. Just walk out, hop in the car, and let your dog process the experience.

Do this as many times as you think you need to. Once or twice a week is a good plan. It probably won't take long for your dog to begin eagerly pulling you through that once-forbidding door.

When a consistent comfort level has been established, try raising the bar a little. Put your dog up on the scale and give treats. If it's okay, take him into an empty exam room and sit there for a minute or two. Even setting him up on the exam table is a fantastic idea. And keep those treats coming. If there is any place that you want your dog to associate with good folks and even better food, the vet's office is that place.

Eventually, of course, reality will have to be faced. Shots will have to be given, blood may have to be drawn, and that hateful thermometer will make its dreaded appearance. But if you have laid the groundwork well, your dog should be much less anxious and much more accepting.

Be ready with those treats. Ideally, work with your vet so that you feed the good stuff while he does the bad stuff. It's wonderful if the assisting staff can offer goodies, too. Timing can be critical here. Also be conscious about not getting in the way. There are some procedures where you'll have to work around each other, such as the Bordetella (or kennel cough) vaccine, which must be squirted directly into the dog's mouth. That makes feeding treats a little awkward, but you can be on standby to fork them over right afterward. And in the case of that nasty thermometer, a steady flow of small and incredible treats will go a long way toward focusing your dog's attention on you, rather than on what's happening at the other end.

You get the idea. Again, do your best to make the good outweigh the bad, and to make the bad not really as bad as it could be.

There will be certain dogs and/or certain procedures which, despite all your good intentions and your best efforts, will become difficult. Those are too individualized for me to address in this general section. You may need to consult a trainer or behaviorist in those tougher cases. Or you may just need to advocate for your dog and ask your vet if he can stop a minute so that you can all take a break and a few deep breaths.

Achieving confidence at the vet can be a long

process. It's okay to back up and rework some areas. It does not mean that you have failed, or that your dog has failed, or that he will never behave appropriately again. What it does mean is that you know where things stand. You know what you need to work on. Care about your dog enough not to give up on him.

It should be clarified that these are suggestions pertaining to routine medical necessities such as shots, nail trimming, ear cleaning, and so on. Obviously, you can't feed treats or tell your vet to back off in an emergency situation. But the idea is to make the routine stuff as stress-free and even enjoyable as possible for your dog. When a more demanding situation does arise, you'll have a foundation of trust and positivity to work from. Your vet and staff will also thank you for your efforts and consideration. Working with a comfortable dog will make their jobs more comfortable, too.

Tip 6

Handling

Everyone pets their dogs, but it's surprising how few people actually handle their dogs. In the last chapter, we talked about teaching your dog to accept handling by a veterinarian. But if your dog isn't accustomed to your own handling, the vet's job is going to be that much harder.

And let's be honest, so is yours. Simple, everyday necessities such as bathing, brushing, trimming nails, and brushing teeth, will be made much easier and more consistent if your dog is okay with you touching sensitive places, like mouth and feet.

Habituating your dog to handling is one of the easiest jobs for you as a caring owner. All you have to do is sit down with him and add a little purpose to your snuggle time.

Dogs tend to be sensitive about their mouths, tails, and paws. Some are also uncertain about having their ears examined. So these are the four areas where you want to focus your attention. Just make it part of the time you already spend stroking and cuddling. Flip over an ear and peek inside. Gently tug on ears and tails. Slip your fingers inside your dog's mouth and lightly rub the gums. And play with paws. Many dogs are nervous and even nippy when it comes to having their nails trimmed. Before it gets to that point, begin desensitizing them by messing with their feet before the nail clippers ever show up. Hold their paws for a little longer than they like, then let go; count their toes; carefully press their nails between your fingers and so on.

As always, puppies are the most receptive candidates for grooming and handling which an older dog might consider intrusive. Just make it a standard part of interaction with them each day.

Take a little more time with older dogs.

Determine what their comfort zone is, and then slowly work to expand that comfort zone. Be nonthreatening and friendly, but don't be passive. If you've identified a problem area, work to overcome it. This doesn't mean being forceful or aggressive, but it does mean not taking "no" for an answer.

I have had very good results with nail-trimming and bathing by giving the dog hard exercise before attempting either task. Wait until your dog is wiped out and sleepy, and then do what needs to be done. With a bath, just scoop the tired dog into the tub without any preamble or persuasion, and then be affirming when he's secured.

"Hey, look at that! What a good boy! That wasn't so bad, was it?"

With nails, I like to take it slower. Often I'll begin by trimming only one or two nails, then putting the clippers away and giving soothing praise. "Very nice job. What a good dog," and so forth. Then I'll run the dog another six or seven miles the next day, wait until he's sacked out afterward, and once again do another couple of toes.

I think the key is to keep things as calm and neutral as possible. Make handling a nonissue. It's just standard procedure. Be gentle but firm. Be reasonable. Don't ask for too much too fast. Keep working on the tough stuff. Offer quiet, gentle praise but not too many treats. Enthusiastic praise or the expectation of treats can make an otherwise mellow dog become too excited for you to finish the job.

If I do have a dog that's particularly difficult about something that we've worked on for a while, I ask for a little more. I make the payoff worth his while. For instance, the dog gets supper only after having a couple of nails trimmed. Or the dog gets to play a long game of fetch with a valued toy after a bath. You know your dog—you pick the reward.

To me, handling is a nonnegotiable. Dogs need to respect and trust their owners enough to allow simple maintenance. But rather than thinking of it as a dominance issue (although in some cases it can be), try to view even the sticking points as an opportunity to bond with your best friend better.

Life is a learning curve. Life with a dog provides both of you with room to grow, adapt, and connect with each other in a way that no other relationship can. And you get some sweet, doggy snuggle time into the bargain.

Tip 7

The Right Tools

It's hard to do good work without good tools.

This is not an exhaustive list, but following are a few of the items that have been most helpful to me and my many dogs over the years. I would never consider bringing a dog, especially a new puppy, into my household without these proven fall-backs to help the process.

❦ Use a Crate.

They're invaluable. A crate provides a safe, homey place for your dog to sleep overnight and to chill and stay out of trouble during the day. It's a tremendous help when you're still working through housetraining.

There are two basic types to choose from: wire and solid-sided plastic. My preference has always been for the plastic variety. They're bulkier and often more expensive than the wire style, but they offer the dog much more privacy than open, wire sides do. Not only do they make a dog feel more secure, but they are also more secure than wire in a physical sense. Wire crates can be easy for a smart, innovative dog to escape from. If you give your dog toys and chews to keep him entertained in a crate, these can also slip through the bars on a wire version, whereas a plastic crate will hold them inside.

Always make the crate a good and rewarding place to be. My dogs eagerly run to their crates when they realize that's where they're supposed to end up. Once again, reach for those high-value treats. Throw a handful of them in ahead of your dog. Add chews, frozen goodies, and interactive toys to the mix.

Remember that the crate is not a punishment or the equivalent of a time-out. It's a safe, reliable refuge for your dog. It is not to be used as a movable prison cell where your dog is incarcerated for the majority of the day and night. Use it judiciously. But use it.

❧No-Chew Spray

This sour stuff is an incredible help, especially when it comes to teething and mischievous puppies. There are several name brands to choose from, made for both indoor and outdoor use. All of them taste and smell extremely bitter. If you catch your puppy ripping up the remote or chomping on the chairs, reach for your deterrent spray and saturate the item. Nine and a half times out of ten, dogs will turn up their noses and think three or four times before attempting that object again.

❧Martingale Collars

These no-slip safety collars are a well-kept secret in the canine world. Please don't walk your dog in a harness. Harnesses were designed to promote pulling. Sled dogs, guide dogs, and dogs trained for tracking all wear harnesses, because those jobs require them to get out in front of their handlers and lean into their task. So, although a harness is much harder for your dog to slip out of, it also enables him to drag you all over the place.

Martingale collars are made to slide loosely over a dog's head and fit comfortably until he tries to do a head twist and slip free. When that happens, the loop to which your leash is attached tightens enough to keep the dog from getting loose. My dogs wear these collars whenever we leave the house, whether we're going for a walk, to the vet, or just for a car ride. They're convenient, comfortable, and very reliable.

Martingales are not designed to prevent pulling. We'll talk about that next. But they prevent leash escapes while still giving you control over your dog's head, which is essential if you're going to be the one in charge and giving direction.

❧ Head Halters

If you do have a dog that pulls, consider either

a Gentle Leader or a Halti. Both of these devices replicate the halters used for horses. Controlling an animal's head gives you control over everything the animal does. Head halters for dogs work via a loop fitted around the muzzle to which your leash is attached. This is not a muzzle in the sense of preventing a dog from nipping. But because pressure and tug are exerted on the dog's facial area, rather than around the neck or chest, it is highly effective to stop pulling, lunging, jumping, or unwanted sniffing.

❧ Retractable Leashes

Like everything else, there are various versions of this contraption. They all operate by allowing the dog to enjoy a much longer leash than the typical five or six feet. Any slack in the leash is taken up by a spring which retracts the extra into a plastic handle held by you. Different lengths and leash styles are available. To me, the longer the better. Longer leashes obviously allow a dog more freedom and exercise, while still keeping him safe and connected to you.

However, there is a time and a place for retractable leashes. If you use one, always be careful and considerate, both of your dog and of those around you. Don't use one in close quarters, like training classes or vet clinics. Retractable leashes are for large, outdoor areas. They're the next best thing to your dog running completely off leash.

❧ Interactive Toys

I mentioned these earlier as wonderful ways to entertain your dog in a crate. There is a whole smorgasbord of choices, ranging from simple to very complex. You can choose from treat balls, puzzle toys, hollow toys to cram with food, and many more variations.

My favorite has always been the rubber Kong toys which can be stuffed with fillers. Squeeze cheese is a fantastic filler for one of these things. Stuff the toy and throw it in the freezer overnight, and your dog will stay busy and happy for quite a while.

❦ Jingles

Because I can't use my eyes to keep track of my multiple dogs, I've learned to be creative about using my ears instead. Every one of my kiddos wears tags, and most of them wear specific bells, too.

Of course, keeping an ID tag on your dog's collar is always a good idea, and adding a rabies tag to that (as required by law in basically every city and state) results in even more jingle. But I've found that, again especially with mischievous puppies who get into everything, adding a lively jingle bell or miniature cowbell can really help to keep tabs on things. Your ears can be where your eyes are not. Learn to use your hearing to keep your baby out of trouble.

Tip 8

Be Consistent

Dogs love routine. Establish one early in the relationship and stick to it. A reliable routine will be a huge help, both to you and to your furry family member, when it comes to feeding, exercise, down time, and even potty training.

However, consistency entails more than just your schedule. It also involves expectations and rules.

Be clear about these before you even bring a new dog home. This is a case where all individuals in the household need to be on the same page. When you have all agreed on what to require of the newest family member, don't be wishy-washy about it.

If you've decided that jumping up on people is not okay, then don't let it happen. Ever. If the house rules are that no dogs are allowed on the furniture, then don't let it happen. Ever.

Don't make excuses for your dog, or for yourself. If you do, you will have a dog that is uncertain or confused. At the very least, a confused dog can result in inconsistent behavior in situations where you really want him to be solid. In a worst-case scenario, it can result in a dog who is unpredictable, domineering, or fearful. If dogs don't know what to expect from you, they will try to create personal stability by making their own rules.

At one of the training clubs I sometimes work with, they have a saying: "One command, one action." In other words, ask for a behavior one time and expect it to happen. If it doesn't happen, then make it happen. Be consistent about what you're wanting and follow through.

No dog is perfect. That isn't the point. All I'm saying is that you need to be as consistent as possible if you expect your dog to be the same.

It's not my job to tell you what rules and expectations to have of your own dog in your own home. What I am telling you is that once you've figured them out, make sure your dog does, too. He needs you to be reliable and consistent just as much as you need him to return the favor.

Tip 9

Pick Your Battles

This is closely related to consistency, but let's approach it from a slightly different angle.

Determine the big, unchangeable, non-negotiable rules of the house, and leave it at that. Don't sweat the small stuff.

Every dog has likes, dislikes, and goofy quirks. And some weird things they do just aren't worth fussing about.

Meg, one of my border collies, has gotten it in her head that whenever I sit down at the kitchen table she needs to jump up from wherever she's hanging out and move. It doesn't matter where she is. She can be right next to me, or at the far end of

Reyna Bradford

the house. But when she hears the scrape of my chair pulled out and my freight settling in, she hops up and transfers herself to somewhere else. It's never to the same place, either.

For years I tried to figure it out. Why was it such a big deal to her that I was sitting down at the table? There was nothing negative associated with it and there was nothing positive associated with it. She never began or ended up in the same place. What exactly was her problem? It bothered me. I wanted to fix it.

So, I made it a project.

For a while, I worked with putting her in a down-stay before I would pull up a chair. I would ask her to lie in the same place each time, and then I would sit down, eat my meal, get up, and then release her. The plan worked in the sense that she wasn't jumping up and wandering the house while I was eating. But after a few weeks, I just decided to drop it.

She wasn't doing anything wrong by getting up and leaving. She wasn't frightened or being naughty. It was just one of those weird things that dogs, and especially border collies, do. So, I left it alone.

You may have to do the same. Remember, dogs are a lot of work. Simply following through with the basic stuff can be challenging enough. Don't make life too complicated for either yourself or your dog. You both try hard.

Tip 10

Use Your Voice

It is a powerful tool. Your voice conveys not only your words, but their meaning and emotional content as well.

Most of us don't need to be convinced that dogs are intuitive. They just seem to get it, and they just seem to get us. Whether it's a livestock guardian dog who somehow senses danger, or a therapy dog who gravitates to the person that needs the most love, dogs often just seem to understand who's who and what's what.

Dogs are real and in the moment. And when you communicate with them, you need to be that way, too.

Don't be phony or fake with your dog. That's particularly true when it comes to your tone of voice.

In this case, I'm a lot more like my dogs than I am like people. I can't see facial expression or body language. Almost everything I absorb through my interactions with other people comes via verbal connection. And it's not just what words are said, but the delivery and tone of voice in which they're said, to which I pay attention.

This is much more true for our dogs than it is even for me. Because, although they do have the ability to see and read expression and body language, dogs lack something essential that I have in spades. While I comprehend every word another person says to me, dogs understand only a very limited vocabulary.

So since they don't process most of your words, be sure you convey meaning through tone of voice.

Praise is crucial to a good, working relationship with a dog, and it needs to be genuine. I don't know how many times I've sat listening to a training class, or ringside at a show, and it's struck me how artificial a handler's praise is. It sounds either put on or else overdone. It may not be scientific, but my experience is that dogs recognize and respond to authenticity. They know when you're faking it.

Be warm and personable when you praise your dog. Bring it out of your heart and not just out of your mouth. Smile and even clap. Pat and rub your dog. You don't have to squeal or talk in a super high voice or talk really fast. In fact, my method of praise is usually to speak more slowly, in a voice perhaps only slightly higher than usual. I speak with warm encouragement, and I throw in familiar phrases that my dogs recognize as "good dog" words.

"Yes!" "What a good girl!" "Very nice job!" "That's right! "Awesome!" and "Good for you!" are some of my favorites, and some of theirs, too.

On the flipside, if you're not happy, you don't have to pretend to be. If my dogs have done something stupid or unacceptable, I let them know about it. I am quick and decisive.

A stern "ah-ah" or "stop it" gets the point across. Verbal corrections should be short and businesslike. Deliver them in a lower, firmer tone of voice than the one you normally use.

Then there are the situations where your dog has already gotten away with something naughty, and you have to pick up the pieces. When I was introducing Snowstorm, one of my Pyrenees guardian dogs, to the group of goats she would be living with, I was offered some unorthodox advice. It came from a lady who worked with Pyrenees rescue, and it's a strategy which I have latched onto and utilized ever since. She told me that if Snowstorm messed up and did something wrong, my response should be to immediately intervene and simply act disgusted. Not to yell or to threaten, but just to take Snowstorm away from the goats, and then to walk away myself. And all the time, she said, I was to talk to Snowstorm in apparent disgust. For example: "I seriously don't have time for this.

What was that all about, anyway? Really? That was totally ridiculous. I guess if that's the way you're gonna be, you're just going to have to leave. Fine. I have better things to do than deal with your nonsense."

It works. Sarcasm and verbal disgust can go a long way toward letting your buddy know you are not happy.

This approach should only be used if you have actually caught your dog in the middle of being bad. It is not effective hours after a mistake has been made. But if I catch my dog in the act, I am still a firm believer in the good, old-fashioned "talking to."

And then for all the companionable, in-between times, just chatter to your dog. Talk about your plans for the day, your latest stress at work, the upcoming weekend with the grandkids, or what you're organizing for supper. Sharing conversation with your dog, albeit one-sided conversation, will make him more aware of and attentive to you. It will get the sound of your normal voice in his ears.

It will invite him in and make him a part of your day and part of your family. He will learn to value your voice. And then, when there really is a reason to correct or to celebrate, your dog will already be in the habit of hearing your voice and understanding what you want.

Mean what you say and say what you mean. Praise with warmth and authenticity. Give verbal corrections with decision and authority. And when you catch your dog just being a brat, it's okay to use the "mean mommy voice."

Your voice is a very effective tool. Use it often and use it well.

Tip 11

Dogs Are Smart

And don't you ever forget it. Dogs have minds, and they know how to use them. They watch us, they study us, and they figure us out. In fact, many times, our dogs train us far better than we train them, and many times they do it far better than we realize.

Consider how dogs just seem to know when it's time to go for a walk, and how they expedite the process. Or how they bring you a favorite toy and get you to toss it, and fifteen minutes later you're still throwing the toy and have missed the first half of your favorite TV show or are almost late for a meeting. Or how they give you that look, and, completely on auto pilot, you obediently reach for the box of dog cookies of which they, of course, already knew the exact location.

But that's the humdrum stuff. There are even more compelling examples than these, including some truly spectacular anecdotes of canine Einsteins.

There is the story of the border collie who masterminded opening the inside door convenient to the family's garage. Grappling and unlatching a slick doorknob would have been stunning enough. But once in the garage, she next contrived how to hop up, hit the right button, and raise the garage door to let herself out into the neighborhood.

Even more impressive is the account of the Afghan hound who turned housebreaker. Apparently, this clever girl would spend the early mornings on the sofa, lazily watching her owners prep for work. Once the humans were out of the house, the dog would hop off the couch, open the front door, arrive at the next-door neighbor's house, and neutralize that door, too. Once safely through that door, she would then make a beeline straight to the refrigerator, pop open that pesky door, and help herself to whatever delicacies might be on offer.

Now that's scary smart.

Your typical dog may not be quite that ingenious. And if we're being brutally honest, some of our dogs may occasionally pull stunts which seem to label them as totally stupid. But my word to the wise still stands.

Dogs are smart.

No matter how they look and no matter how they behave, never lose sight of that fact. They learn our routines, learn our words, learn our body language. They learn our expectations and our family and friendship dynamics. They tune into when we're tired or distracted or not paying attention. They anticipate.

For your part, you need to learn, first of all, what remarkable sponges dogs really are. Even the ones that seem more zany than they do brainy are still soaking things in.

Learn to think one step ahead of your dog. Or better yet, two or three steps ahead. When it comes to positive behavior, I anticipate it, support it, and then am ready to reward it.

When it comes to negative behavior, I like to stop it before it even starts. To do that, you need to pay attention. You need to read the situation. Learn to understand how your dog thinks, absorbs information, and reacts to it. Then you react to it before he does.

My mini golden doodle, Butterscotch, is a very high-energy, playful guy. He is also young—not quite a year and a half old. So, he's a teenage boy with a ton of run in his system, and he also really likes other dogs. There are at least two dogs who live near us that enjoy chasing cars. And although Scotch hasn't developed that dangerous habit himself, he does like to chase them as they chase the cars.

Obviously, this is not a good option, either. It's one of those battles we talked about earlier. I've chosen to take issue with it, be firm about it, and stand my ground. My dogs do not chase either cars or other dogs. End of discussion.

So, I've had to learn to anticipate the sequence of events. If I hear one of those neighbor dogs barking, or if my own dogs start acting squirrely and clue me in that one of the car-chasers is patrolling the road, I begin to keep Scotch closer to me. If a car happens along at just the wrong moment, I get him right next to me with a fistful of treats and a good grip on his collar. And then, once the car has gone by and the neighbor dog is still running with it, I continue to keep him with me.

In other words, I do not wait until the car and the neighbor dog have flashed past us and my own teenage terror is barreling down the road at thirty miles an hour before I begin screaming and threatening. I think ahead, put the pieces together, and intuit what Scotch is going to try getting away with. Then I stop it before it has a chance to get started.

Learn what motivates your dog. Lots of dogs who are blamed for being "stupid" are actually not properly motivated. When compared to the pleasures of forbidden food, other dogs, new people, or an escape from the yard, we owners can be pretty boring. Find the right treats, the right tone of voice, or even the right equipment. What does your dog value and what captures and keeps his attention?

Now we're going to talk down and dirty for a minute. As the mature and responsible human in this unique dog-and-human relationship, you need to realize that you're beloved dog—no matter how sweet and special and adorable that dog may be—does not always have your best interests at heart. Dogs can be very calculating, manipulative, and eager to take advantage of you any way they can. In a word, they can be brats.

Trust me, as a blind individual who has lived with many of them for many years—I know. My dogs clearly understand that I can't see, and they have no qualms about working the system. It's my constant job to stay those three steps ahead of them indoors and out, in the ring and outside of it, on walks, on trips, or even just on the couch.

Accept this about your own dog. While they can be incredibly caring, attentive, and even altruistic at times, dogs do have their own agenda. Be aware of what it is at all times, and don't let them get away with nonsense.

The good news is that, because dogs are so clever, yours will learn to play by your rules fairly fast as long as you do the legwork.

A case in point is my miniature Australian shepherd, Brio. Of all the dogs I currently have, Brio is the smartest. And not only is she smart, but she is bossy and manipulative to boot. A few years ago, she and several other of my herding breeds were getting really naughty about rushing the front gate. The games would begin every time we came home from our long, daily walks. Four or five of my doggy entourage would charge down the driveway ahead of me until they reached the closed front gate. I would arrive a minute or two later, by which time they would be fixated on the latch, jammed together with their noses glued to the tiny opening between the gate and the post. I would unlatch the gate, crack it open about half an inch, and like lightning, they would slam their way through, snarling and snapping and getting right in each other's faces.

Being the smallest of the bunch, Brio usually managed to squirt through first. She would then get right under everyone else's feet, biting and barking in all her bossy Aussie outrage, and endeavoring to turn the thundering herd in a different direction.

I decided that it was ridiculous. This new game was way too snarky and too assertive, and it was going to lead to a nasty squabble before too long.

So, I put a stop to it. Rather than allowing them to get to the gate before I did, I positioned each of the dogs in a sit-stay twenty or thirty yards back up the driveway. It became our "wait at the gate" exercise. Only after I opened the gate and gave the release word could they come streaking down the remainder of the driveway, through a gate that was now wide open and therefore no longer a flash point.

It worked the first time. But by the second time, Brio had wised up. She hung back respectfully while I situated the other offenders, and then, before I could turn to collect her, she had skipped down to the yard gate, located the only hole in the fence, and zipped through to the other side. Now in the front yard, she would have a bull's-eye shot at each of the others as they came tearing through once the gate was opened.

Nope, not on my watch. I called her back through the gate, got her by the collar, and settled her in a position well behind the others. I told her to wait there and let her know I meant it. And then we went back to square one, and I began opening the gate again.

I could share story after story, but you get the point. Dogs are smart.

They know us pretty well, and they're not always on our team. Your job is to be savvy enough, creative enough, and determined enough to keep them honest. In short, you actually do need to be smarter than your dog.

Tip 12
Cultivate a Sense of Humor

In the next few chapters, we're going to dive in and get more specific about some actual training methods that I've found to be helpful. But before that, let's do a reality check.

Training dogs to behave well, and teaching them to be good members of the family, is hard work. But it shouldn't be boring or rigorous work. Dogs love to have fun, and you need to enter into the spirit of the thing and have fun right along with them. Here's another word to the wise: A sense of humor will carry both you and your dog a long way. If you're going to be an effective trainer, learning to laugh at yourself is a critical life skill.

Dogs keep you humble. Everyone who trains for any kind of competitive canine sport or performance event has heard and has probably even said that phrase more than once. Dogs are not robots or furry automatons. And, to make things even more interesting, they have definite humor of their own.

Case in point: my Australian shepherd, Mesa. She has been gone for many years now, but one of her stunts still lives in infamy. Up until Mesa, I had tinkered around with dogs in the competition obedience ring, but we had never gone anywhere much. We had earned novice titles, and we had played around with rally, a sport closely related to obedience and largely comprised of heelwork. By the time Mesa came on the scene, I knew I was totally hooked on the ring thing. I wanted a dog that I could take places, a dog that could take me places, and she was the one.

She was a trim, amber-eyed blue merle, and she was eager and smart. I had set my heart on earning the Companion Dog Excellent title with her. This is an advanced obedience title, awarded by the

American Kennel Club, and it was a higher honor than any of my other dogs had ever achieved. Earning it was a definite challenge.

To earn a CDX, the dog must do everything off leash. There are jumping and retrieving exercises, and there is no room for error. No re-tries, no double commands, no mistakes allowed.

And Mesa and I got it.

I was absolutely thrilled, and so was my dad, who had persevered through all of our efforts, driven us to shows and training venues, and put up with my fussing in between. Part of my bargain with him was that, for every title I earned in the ring, he would receive a homemade apple pie. I mean—let's be honest—without his help and driving skills, Mesa and I never would have left the front yard.

So, I made him a pie. And then, just because I was in a celebratory mood, I made myself a pie, too.

They came out of the oven steaming hot and golden-brown. The whole house smelled good. I set them on cooling racks, pushed them far back on the kitchen table, and then went outdoors for a few minutes to do something else.

When I came back in, Mesa had vanished. So had the pies. Both of them.

It didn't take a rocket scientist to figure out the sequence of events. Mesa, left to her own devices and obviously also happy to celebrate, had vaulted onto the table and put those pies in a better place. It was her achievement we were celebrating, after all. What was the problem?

Okay, of course I know she wasn't really thinking things through quite that eloquently. But the irony was hardly lost on me. I had worked my hiney off earning that special title. It was an obedience title no less, with exercises designed to demonstrate just how well-trained a good dog could be. And the very one who had earned it with me then turned around and was a very bad dog.

A sense of humor is crucial.

Dogs can be naughty, and they can also just be nutty. Tassie, my smooth-coated collie, once pulled the bed sheets through the baby gate which blocks the door to my bedroom. I had just stripped the sheets off the bed, and was in the process of fitting fresh ones, when I noticed one of the dirty sheets inching its way out of the room. By the time I got there, Tassie had reeled at least half of it through the bars and into the hallway.

Tassie also has a couple of jokes she pulls while waiting for me to leave the house and head out on our daily walks. One of them involves elicit substances. She is just the right size to slink between the post and the latched gate into our miniature donkey's corral. This area is off limits to dogs—first of all, because donkeys do not like dogs, and this one has been aggressive toward them in the past. And second of all, because I really don't want my dogs eating donkey poop, of which there is always a ready supply in the corral. Tassie won't touch it if I'm in the yard. But, while I'm still in the house, she sneaks into the corral, chomps down as much poop as she can grab, and then dashes back out of the corral and up the driveway as soon as I step out on the front patio.

It's a great trick for her to play on Mom. I've learned to bungee the corral gate tightly shut.

Then there's Scotch, who is one of the goofiest dogs I have ever lived with. He just does silly stuff. He spins in circles and jumps in the air on every walk we take. He loves to paddle and splash in every wet ditch or puddle we encounter. He loves stomping through the ice if any puddles are frozen. He loves snow. He violently wags his tail just because I walk into the same room with him.

There have been scientific studies conducted which seem to indicate that dogs actually have the ability to laugh. The happy, huffing sounds that many of them make when playing, either with us or with other dogs, have been interpreted by some behaviorists as canine laughter.

Whether or not they really do laugh, let your dog teach you to do it more yourself. They are some of the happiest creatures on the planet. Learn to appreciate their uniqueness, their individuality, and their silliness. Learn to enjoy their joy.

Of course, as discussed in the previous chapter, not everything they find funny really is funny or acceptable in our human society. I'm not suggesting that you let them do anything they want just because they enjoy it. As I said before, don't let your dog get away with nonsense. Dogs can be extremely good at being extremely bad. There will come a time in your beautiful relationship when you will truly want to strangle your best furry buddy.

You will get frustrated, and you will get discouraged. But don't let it ruin your day, or your relationship. Be a good sport. Pick up the pieces, take a few steps back, learn from your dog's mistakes, and from your own mistakes. Be determined, but don't be angry. Life is too short, and our dogs' lives are even shorter. And if you're going to be a serious trainer, you're going to have to learn to laugh.

Tip 13

Chose the Right Chews

Dogs need to chew. Everyone knows about puppies and their legendary months of teething. But even as adults, most dogs still have a natural desire to chew, and some will continue to do it well into their senior years.

Providing appropriate objects for your dog to seek and destroy will give both of you some peace of mind. Your dog will be able to satisfy the inborn drive to rip and shred, while you can be much more confident that he's leaving your furniture and shoes intact.

Offer teething puppies a wide variety of chewy toys. These do not include plush squeaky toys nor knotted rope toys. Although some puppies really get down with those, both these types of toys can become hazardous as they disintegrate. Some puppies are careful about not actually ingesting what they chew, but that certainly doesn't extend to all of them. Globs of stuffing and long threads and fibers from rope toys are not items that you want fouling up your baby's digestive system. So, keep these toys out of reach unless under special supervision. Not only can those softer toys become hazards, but in addition, they do not provide a puppy with the opportunity for rigorous chewing. Teething puppies especially need harder, more resistant surfaces to gnaw on.

There are a myriad of styles, textures, shapes, and edibilities to pick from. Below are a few of my dogs' favorite chews.

❧Beef Hooves

These have proven invaluable to me and my pack over the years. I keep two or three of them lying around the floor at all times, and even many of my adult dogs still enjoy them. Hooves are high-value enough to keep a dog interested for an extended period of time, but not so high-value that they precipitate food fights. They are edible, but it takes a lot of work for a dog to gnaw them down.

❧ Rawhide Chips

These are roughly rectangular pieces of rawhide, cut in various sizes and thicknesses. They're usually basted in either chicken or beef, which makes them extra appealing. These are a little higher value than hooves, and I only dole them out to dogs that are in crates, rather than leaving them free-choice around the premises. They don't last as long as hooves do, but they usually keep a dog's interest more readily.

❧ Nilabones

These solid, bone-shaped chews are not edible, but they are infused with dog-friendly flavors to encourage chewing. Some dogs like them and some have no idea what to do with them. These are usually safe to leave scattered around the house, since they aren't as tempting to every dog and won't result in skirmishes.

There are also chews available which are similar to Nilabones but which are edible. These are also worth trying, since they're very tasty and rewarding, while still taking some time for a puppy to work through.

❧ Pig Ears and Bully Sticks

These are gross, but you're not the one chewing on them. Most dogs love these stinky goodies. The pig ears don't last very long for most chewers, but they do provide a diversion and some busy crunch time. The bully sticks last longer and can be bought in various sizes.

❧ Butcher Bones

Very few dogs will turn these down. Butcher bones, or soup bones, are the gold standard when you're talking chewy choices.

The best kind are those purchased from an actual meat processing facility. Throw them in the freezer overnight and give your dog the extra challenge of gnawing through cold and frozen texture.

If you're not up to your dog's toys being quite this graphic, bones can be bought at pet supply stores and supermarkets. They're a little cleaner and less gory packaged this way, which your dog might not appreciate, but which may make offering them more palatable for you. My dogs seem to do best with the knuckle bones, which offer more of a chance to really get their teeth in and wrestle with the prize.

However, if you do use butcher bones, be forewarned. These grisly delicacies are extremely high-value to almost every dog. They are treasures which I would recommend giving only in a crate or in a closed room, separate from any other animals. Even sweet and tolerant dogs can become very possessive over meaty bones. Be smart and judicious about when and how you offer them.

There are tons more chewing options available, and both you and your dog can have some fun exploring them and finding out what works the best. Set out a wide range of them for your puppy and watch to see what happens. It's fascinating how individual dogs really do have individual tastes and preferences.

Having the right chew toys underfoot will help your puppy to teethe effectively and appropriately. It will keep your teenage dog out of trouble. And it will allow your adult dog to still relish the satisfaction of getting his jaws around something he enjoys, and which you definitely won't miss when it's gone.

Tip 14
Learn to Play the Trade Game

Your dog has stolen something off limits. Something he's not supposed to have, and something he really wants. The way it usually works is that he leads you on a rousing chase, all around the house and/or yard. Chairs get toppled. Lamps hit the floor. Maybe even people hit the floor. And all the while, your merry little miscreant dashes delightedly just one or two steps ahead of you, flaunting the forbidden item and staying inches out of reach.

It also usually happens that this inconvenience occurs just before you have to go somewhere, and it most often centers on an item that is either hazardous to the dog, or else outright embarrassing to you.

If you haven't been there already, you will be. It's just part of living with dogs.

So how do you flip the situation in order that your dog ends up playing your game instead of his own naughty version?

The pivotal concept is to offer your dog a prize far better than the one he's running off with. The kicker is, if he wants it, he has to give up the off-limits item and let you take it first. In other words, you're working out a trade.

So, your dog has just snitched something he's not supposed to have. You see it, he catches your eye and stands poised, ready for the fun to begin. This is where you need to step up and be smarter than your dog.

The immediate and best response from you is simple: stationary quiet. As much as you may desperately want to, do not chase. For one thing, it's what your dog wants from you and it will only reinforce the naughty behavior. For another thing, you will almost never catch your dog until either the damage has been done to the item in question, or else until your dog decides he's tired of the game and lets you get close. In either case, the game has gone on too long, and we all know who has really won.

Instead of chasing, stand still. Then, when your dog realizes things are not going quite according to plan, turn around and walk to wherever you keep your bribery materials.

Think scrumptious on this one. Dogs are extremely savvy at assessing value. If your puppy is tucking into a big bar of chocolate or diving into a dirty diaper, a plain old dog biscuit probably isn't going to cut it. You need to go for the good stuff.

This is once again where you reach for the messy, stinky treats. Canned meats, deli meats, or cooked chicken will usually do the trick. Draw your dog's attention to you as you walk away. Smack your lips, pat your thigh, clap your hands. Add in a word or phrase so that he knows something good is on the way. All of my dogs know the line, "You wanna cookie?" and will transfer their attention to me immediately upon hearing it.

Continue talking up the goodies as you get to the fridge or cabinet. Use an excited tone of voice, drop in that treat word every chance you get, and make all kinds of noise getting the stuff out.

By this point, your dog should be right with you. But just in case he hasn't wised up yet, there's nothing wrong with bringing the treats to him for the first time or two. You want him to know exactly what he's missing by holding onto that forbidden but extremely boring item which started it all.

Whether your dog is already with you, or whether you've had to track him down, make sure you catch his attention. Then, wave a big handful of yummies under his nose and say that phrase like you mean it: "Hey, buddy, you wanna cookie?"

Most dogs will drop the bad item and come right to the handful of treats. But before handing them over, play your part of the game. First, pick up the article your dog was not supposed to have.

Make sure he can't grab it back from you, and then dole out the treats.

If your dog still isn't convinced and wants to hang onto the forbidden item, there are a couple courses of action you can take, depending on what the item is. If it's something that he just wants to play with—for instance, your cell phone or a pair of underpants filched from the laundry—go ahead and remove it from his mouth. Then immediately pop your handful of goodness into his jaws instead. If, however, your dog has something very high-value—for example, a meaty butcher bone—things get a little dicey.

My strategy in cases like this is to never let my dog win. I said he can't have it, and I'm going to make sure I get it back. But obviously, getting nipped is not an acceptable option, either. Make sure that your dog sees and smells what you're offering as a trade. Then, begin dropping it on the floor nearby. Say things like, "Look! What's this?" or "Wow, look what I've got!"

Most dogs can't resist in a situation like that. When he drops the bone and begins cleaning up the floor, casually pick the bone up and remove it from the area. I would also recommend that once the bone is gone and the floor is polished, you call your dog to you two or three more times and give the same awesome treats out of your hand. Have your dog sit or lie down before taking them and encourage him to follow you to another room between helpings. This will redirect his attention onto you and away from the trophy that was lost. It will also subtly but indisputably confirm you as the leader and provider and your dog as the follower who takes cues from you.

A few adult dogs will have food aggression issues. That's something you should ultimately tackle with a reputable trainer. But this is the groundwork. Show your dog that you have something better, but that the only way it's attainable is by playing your game.

For those dogs who just won't capitulate and come to get the treats, your best plan is to eliminate options. Close doors so that he's confined to one room. Get other people or animals out of the way so that your dog cannot involve them in the mischief. And when the options and escape routes are closed, once again offer up your trade.

It can be a little tougher to play the trade game outdoors, farther away from the fridge, and with more running room for your four-legged thief. But the same principles apply. Don't chase. Encourage your dog to pay attention to and follow you. Use your cookie phrase excitedly and often. And both of you should end up in the house, and most likely in the kitchen. Again, you may actually need to bring the goodies outdoors for the first time or two. But your dog will figure it out.

There's a lot of power in the trade game. It's non-confrontational, while still establishing you as the leader in the relationship. It teaches your dog that you make and reinforce the rules, but that in so doing, you are also the giver of good things. And let's be honest: it usually keeps diapers, cell phones, and underpants from eternal destruction while also keeping your best friend safe from occasional hazards.

I may have said it before, but the way to a dog's heart is through a dog's stomach. It always pays to remember that. And in this case, it pays both you and your dog.

Tip 15

Nothing In Life Is Free

When it comes to your dog, being fed is not a right. It is a privilege.

Simply plunking down a food-filled bowl twice every day is one of the sloppiest and laziest things you can do as a responsible owner. Free-feeding your dog is even worse. Your dog needs to earn that daily ration. He is not entitled to it. It is not automatically his just because he has a cute face or just because you've had a hard day. Owning a dog is a twenty-four seven commitment, and that is especially true when it comes to feeding time.

To a dog, there are few things, if anything, more important than food. Dogs love food, live for food, and long for food. And, as the provider of this unspeakable treasure, you are in the ideal position to leverage that love and longing for the good of both you and your furry companion. Take full advantage of it and use that leverage.

Make your dog work for his portions. This will establish you as the loving and consistent leader which your dog needs, and it will give you confidence and authority in the relationship. It's one of the best things you can do to ensure that both of you recognize your individual roles in the household.

But this is not just an "alpha" thing. Asking your dog to work for food will also encourage your dog to learn. Not eating unless he works is a strong and positive motivator, and your dog will gobble up the subsequent learning in more ways than one.

Let's begin with breakfast. Instead of just dumping kibble into the dish and shoving it under your dog's nose, carry the bowl to the spot where you typically feed and ask him to sit. When his bottom hits the floor, wait three or four seconds while quietly praising the sit. Then gently lower the dish. If your dog starts to get up, stand up yourself, raising the dish out of reach, and repeat the sit command. Do this as many times as it takes. No sit, no food. Absolutely no exceptions. Your dog is only allowed to eat when he has held the sit, made eye contact with you, and finally been released to eat.

This would be a good time to choose a release word if you haven't done so already. Your dog needs to know when it's okay to break the sit position (or any other position you've requested) and begin eating. So, pick a definite word to signal that it's okay to chow down or goof off. My dogs know the word "recess" as their release word. It's quick and original and it's not a word they hear anywhere else or from anyone else. You can use something like "free time," "all done," or anything else you choose, as long as it is not a common word or one that cues another behavior. Your release word only and always means that your dog is officially off duty and can go do what he wants.

Eye contact is important, too. Don't release your dog and let him dive into the dish if he is staring at the bowl or avoiding your gaze for any other reason. You are the important one in this situation. The food is secondary. It comes from you, as does the okay to eat it. Your dog needs to look to you for direction, not rivet his attention on the stuff in your hand.

Once he's competent with a sit, try asking for a "down" before allowing your dog to eat. The same rules apply. No breaking the position until you say so, even when the bowl is on the floor right in front of his toes. Keeping good eye contact with you and waiting for that magic release word before bolting down breakfast also remains unchanged. If any of those things are compromised, pick up the bowl and start over.

This ritual can become as elaborate as you decide it should be. Sometimes, a basic sit will suffice. Other times, you might choose to work through an entire training session before a meal. On the morning of a show, my dogs do not get their food until after they've competed and come out of the ring.

Moving on throughout the day, continue to think about the goodies and treats you give. These, too, should never be tossed out lightly. They may not be as essential as an actual meal, but they are often tastier and therefore of higher value than standard, bland kibble. Remember, dogs are experts at assessing value. So, if I'm handing out a salmon brownie or a cube of tuna fudge, my dog is going to have to earn it.

Have fun with this. You don't have to get out the training gear or run to the nearest agility obstacle. Think of things you can do quickly in the house. Teach your dog tricks. My dogs can do everything from a basic "shake hands" to complex skills like opening drawers or pulling off my slippers. The sky is the limit here. Work for food is not just about leadership and old-school dominance. It's about bonding with your best friend and having a good time, while still reminding your dog that you are in charge and that you call the shots. And that's a good place for both of you to be. Your dog will trust you more and learn to look to you for direction, and you yourself will become more confident, more creative, and more positive.

By the time you get to supper, nothing has changed. Once again ask for attention, eye contact, and whatever skill you decide to work with. Many times, working on a command or behavior that tends to be a sticking point for your dog can yield the best results before an anticipated meal. If your obedience dog isn't sure that retrieving the dumbbell is a great idea, ask for three or four decent retrieves before offering the supper menu. If your agility prospect is freaked out by the teeter-totter, run him over that obstacle several times and get good and happy before clunking down the kibble. Make feeding time count.

Finally, what if you're someone who is not interested in canine competition at all, but who just wants a dog to hang out with around the house? Sorry, you're not off the hook, either. Providing food to a dog only when that dog is well-behaved and respectful can go miles toward transferring the same attitude to everyday interactions around the house and neighborhood. Work on this. For instance, if your dog goes crazy when the doorbell rings, set it up so that you or someone you know rings that doorbell just before feeding time, and let your dog know the food will not be available until there is quiet. Evaluate your dog and pick whatever problem area you become aware of and use that daily food ration as training gold.

And if you have a dog that's just plain awesome and doesn't need to work on anything at all, so what? Don't be lazy, and don't let your dog get lazy, either. Your relationship is more crucial than the actual practice sessions. Enhancing and maintaining that relationship is what's most important and doing so via food is the most effective method.

It's worth noting that another variation is to get rid of the bowl entirely. Instead, you can feed your dog out of your pocket all day long. Every morning, measure out your dog's food portion for the whole day. Then carry it in a bait bag belted around your waist or tuck the baggie of kibble into your pants pocket and keep it with you. Then as the day goes on, slowly ration out the food whenever and wherever you need to.

This strategy can work even better than feeding from a bowl, since your dog will never be looking for one. The food will only ever come from your hand. Therefore, your dog's attention is even more intently focused on you and whatever your next request might be.

I especially like this game plan for two types of dogs. The first is for those dogs who tend to be very pushy and dominant. If you have an adult rescue who can act a little snarky, feeding out of your pocket will gain respect faster than almost anything else you can try. You have the food, you have the power, and you will gain the respect. It will take only a minimal amount of time before your dominant dog steps back and lets you run the show.

The second group of dogs that this strategy really benefits are those who already work for a living all day long. Certain types of assistance canines fall into this category, as do some types of specially trained working dogs, such as arson detection canines. For these special dogs, the daily ration of kibble often serves as both their sustenance and as their reward.

I've had to learn it, you've had to learn it, and now it's your dog's turn to figure it out. If he wants it, he'll work for it. After all, nothing in life is free.

Tip 16
Be Smart About
Giving Treats

It should go without saying, especially after the previous chapter, that paying attention to how many treats you give your dog is a must.

Treats are extra. They are a bonus. Sure, they're nice to fork over every once in a while, but they are not necessary. Besides, if you're really honest, how much of dropping a dog cookie into those drooling jaws is about the momentary pleasure it affords your dog, and how much is really about the longer-lasting feel-good factor that it affords to you?

Be careful not to fall into the trap of giving out of guilt. It's easy to do.

Examples: "We didn't have time to go for a walk today, so you can have a cookie instead." Or, "I know mommy hasn't been home all day long, so here's a treat for the cute baby to make up for it."

Lavishing goodies out of a sense of guilt never solves anything. Especially when it comes to a dog.

And there's an even more insidious problem. Obviously, piling on the treats can rapidly result in your dog piling on the pounds. Most dog treats are crammed with calories. And unless you're going to expend the additional effort to fight the battle of the doggy bulge, you need to limit your love to just a couple cookies per day. There is such a thing as too much generosity.

However, this chapter is intended to address more than just the issue of offering too many treats. Because, let's face it, there will come a time and a place when palming over a bonus to your best friend is one hundred percent okay. And when that time comes, here are some things to consider.

The type of treat you actually choose to dole out is a question worth pondering. With such an overwhelming array of choices on the market, it can be quite a challenge. Treats come in so many flavors, shapes, sizes, textures, packagings, colors, quantities and qualities, that the task of selecting just two or three bags or boxes to bring home can be staggering.

My personal preference is to go with treats that are small and soft. Bite-size is usually best. That way you can pop the munchy in your dog's mouth and know that it's going to disappear quickly, with a minimum of mess and crumbs. Soft treats are easy for a dog to chew and swallow, meaning that the dog's attention can be swiftly transferred back to you, or to your family, or friends. This is especially important if you're using the treat for training purposes.

Hard, crunchy cookies take longer for a dog to dispose of. There's nothing necessarily wrong with that, but just be conscious of both when and where you give them. Crunchy treats can crumble or break. If you have multiple dogs in one kitchen, as I do, the dog receiving the cookie may not be excited about sharing those falling fragments with other pack members. Large, hard biscuits that require more chew time also encourage some dogs to go off and hide while they finish the prize. This, in turn, can then encourage other resident dogs, cats, or even children, to follow behind and bother or bully the dog who is trying to eat in private. None of those are good situations.

Plan to offer those larger biscuit-type treats only at certain times. For example, when it's bedtime and you're putting your dog in a crate or a certain room for the night, giving a chunky biscuit is fine. There's no pressure for your dog to finish the treat fast, there is ample privacy, and by the time the dog is done, you're out of the picture and the lights have probably been turned off.

Another situation when big biscuits are beneficial might be when you're leaving the house without your dog for a few hours. Again, the idea is to stow your dog in whatever safe place you've chosen for him to stay while you're away, and then to hand over a cookie or two that will take some chewing and provide some distraction. Once the goodies are gone, you will be, too.

Another thing to consider is the shape of the treats you give. Long, stick-like yummies—such as Pupperoni or jerky treats—are very popular for dogs. However, be aware that, unless you have a huge dog with an enormous mouth, those treats are too long to be taken in one bite. The result is that the treat is chomped in half, the bottom half hits the floor, and if you have other animals underfoot, it won't stay on the floor for long. This is a situation just begging for a fight to flare up. Avoid it by either breaking the sticks into smaller pieces or else only giving them when you know your dog won't be harassed.

In the case of multiple-dog households, do not allow bullying, and do not show favoritism. Supervise while your dogs devour their treats. In my house, pushing, posturing, and growling at treat time is never allowed. No dog is favored with more treats than any other dog.

Also, for those of you with multiple dogs, vary the order in which you give out treats. In my home, no one dog is any more or any less special than any other dog. There is no cookie hierarchy in my household. The dog who gets the first treat should be the dog who is acting the calmest and the most polite.

Additionally, try not to allow your dog to snap cookies out of your hand. My rule is that if I feel teeth on my fingers, that's too much mouth. Be calm and deliberate about handing over a cookie. Offer it in a loose fist first, and if you feel teeth, clench your hand and pull it away. Tell your dog something like "be gentle," pause to let it process, and then offer the treat again. When your dog is polite and doesn't grab at your hand or fingers, give the goody on an open palm, similar to the way you would feed a horse.

It's totally normal for your dog to be excited and eager about taking a treat from you. Treats are awesome and tasty, and they mix up the humdrum routine of an average day. But don't let the excitement get to the stage where your fingers are crunched or compromised. No one likes a grabby, mouthy dog.

When it comes to a big responsibility like owning a dog, sometimes it's the little responsibilities that really count. Giving treats falls into that category. Be smart about it. Treat time is a good time. Let's make sure it stays that way.

Tip 17

Train on the Fly

It's always a good plan to carry treats in your pocket.

One of the key components to effective training is not just to reward good behavior, but to reward it immediately. Heartfelt, verbal praise is one way to do that, but there's no substitute for food when it comes to getting and shaping the behaviors that you want.

The window of time to reward something good that your dog does is about three seconds. Tops. That is the minuscule amount of time you have between your dog doing something right, and you handing over a treat to say so. Three seconds. Any longer than that, and your dog is much less likely to make the connection and recall the right behavior.

Needless to say, three seconds doesn't give you much wiggle room. It's not exactly enough time for you to race back to the fridge, fumble through the contents, locate something dog-appropriate and amazing, gallop back to your furry friend, and pop it in his mouth with an out-of-breath, "Yes, what a good dog!"

Furthermore, many times you and your dog aren't anywhere near the home place when you need to give a quick reward. And particularly, when it comes to a new puppy or a rambunctious rescue, rewarding the right behavior immediately is something you can't afford to skip.

Formal training sessions are essential. There should always be times, especially for those of you who plan to pursue performance events with your dog, when you'll have planned and programmed training outings. But what about between times? What about when you're outside on a walk, or when your neighbor stops by unexpectedly, and both times your dog remembers what you've been working on and does the right thing? You better have more than just an insipid "good dog" to throw at him.

The solution is to train on the fly. Always be forearmed and ready with rewards. Keep treats in your pocket during the day and look for opportunities to use them. (You can also use a bait bag, but be advised that wearing one for an entire day can be cumbersome.)

Much like the work-for-food program outlined earlier, pocket treats will keep your dog's attention more closely focused on you. Your dog knows you have them. And as the days unfold, he'll also learn that there's a good chance he'll end up getting them if he can just figure out how.

A dog's stomach is not only the way to a dog's heart. Most of the time, it's the way to a dog's mind as well. As you begin to make it a habit to watch for and reward positive behavior, your dog will look to you more and more. He will try hard to please you and to get those pocket treats, and the two of you will become an even tighter team.

Treats in your pocket make immediate delivery possible. You'll be ready to reward on a moment's notice, no matter what the situation or circumstance.

Having treats readily accessible in your pocket can make it much easier for a puppy or a totally clueless rescue to understand the concept of appropriate potty habits. After all, house-training can be hard. This is especially true if you need your dog to potty reliably in many different environments, such as rest areas or show venues. However, bestowing a goody as soon as business has been taken care of goes a long way toward establishing acceptable potty behavior. You can even teach your dog to eliminate on command, a skill which can be invaluable in some situations. Keep those cookies close and be ready to hand them over as soon as your puppy does the necessary.

Quick treats are indispensable when it comes to socialization encounters. Teaching your dog to ignore other dogs, or not to bother busy people, or to power through scary stuff like loud noises and visual startles is much tougher to do without cookies in hand. Be ready to reassure, redirect, and reward whenever the two of you step into the big, wide world. Prepare your pocket and get out there.

A final, fun plus of carrying treats is that you can catch and validate behaviors that you may want from your dog, but which may be hard to teach. This is most applicable when it comes to training certain tricks. Sometimes, instead of luring and coaxing and posing, the best method is to catch your dog in the act and quickly reward. If there's a specific, natural behavior that you want to teach as a trick, (for instance, the "take a bow" or the "shake it off" commands), be ready for it and pop that treat as soon as you see it. Watch for desired behavior and then be immediately ready to reach in your pocket and reward.

Perfect pocket treats can be a challenge to choose. They should be small; small enough for lots of them to fit comfortably in your pocket and small enough for your dog to gulp them down quickly.

However, they should be substantial enough that your dog wants them and will work for them. Think tiny but mighty. They should also be soft so as not to require much chewing, but not so soft that they crumble in the close quarters of a pants pocket.

As usual, there are many and myriad options from which to make your selection. Take some time to look and to experiment. Find out which varieties work best in your particular pocket, and which of those varieties your dog most seems to appreciate.

I generally keep two or three different kinds of treats floating around in my pocket through an average day. Dogs do like variation. It's fun for them to wonder exactly what you'll pull out and hand over next time they get it right.

So, stock up your pocket each morning, and watch for your best friend to be on his best behavior. It will happen, and when it does, you need to be ready.

Tip 18

Teach A Reliable Recall

There is nothing more necessary, more important, or more essential that you can train your dog to do than to come when you call.

Coming to you on command can keep curious canines out of all kinds of trouble—both from getting into it and from causing it. A solid recall can prevent your dog from getting up on the counter, from chasing the cat, and from visiting the neighbor's kids when they all have dripping ice cream cones. It can bring him back from an encounter with an unfriendly dog, or from one with an unfriendly person, or from dashing straight into the middle of traffic. A reliable recall can be very convenient. And it can also save your dog's life.

Over the last few chapters, I have offered lots of advice and various training techniques. But this is the only time I'm going to actually insist that you train your dog to learn a specific command. Whatever lifestyle you have, and whatever breed you choose to share it with, you absolutely must teach your dog to come when you call.

Start small and start with the right attitude. Don't stress, and don't be demanding. First and foremost, this training needs to be fun.

Begin with your dog's name.

Most dogs learn their names more or less by osmosis. Use it enough in connection with them, and they figure it out. However, your personal job is to teach your dog's name intentionally and to do it in a positive manner.

Your dog should associate his name only with good things. This may not be realistic for the entire rest of his life. But try very hard, especially for the first week or two, never to use your dog's name in conjunction with anything except praise and affection.

If you catch your furkid being bad, don't instantly holler his name and dole out discipline. Rap out a sharp "ah ah!" or "leave it!" for example, to get the attention and stop the behavior. Do not use your dog's name as a correction.

Teaching name recognition, and doing so with positive association, is as simple as—once again—reaching for the goody bag. Get your dog in a familiar environment with no distractions. Scoop out a handful of treats. Be sure your dog is right beside you and then say the name.

Give a treat. It doesn't matter if your dog is paying attention to you or not. He will be within a few seconds.

Say your dog's name, give a treat. Say your dog's name, give a treat.

Name, treat. Name, treat. And keep doing it. As your dog catches on, begin stepping away as you say the name so that your dog automatically follows you. He is actually already coming when you call, although neither one of you realizes it yet.

Keep the sessions short but repeat them several times per day. Resist the temptation to progress too quickly. As simple and obvious as this game may seem, you want a concrete and unshakable connection to be formed in your dog's mind. You're establishing a new habit. You say his name, and food follows. Every time.

As before, pull out the A-plus treats for this exercise. Tiny pieces of incredible goodness, and your dog gets every one of them, if he just comes to your hand when you say his name.

After two or three days of this, begin to mix things up a little bit. Call your dog's name from across the room when it's not expected, making sure to already have a treat in hand. Do this at odd times. Do it in odd places, like out in the yard or in a completely different part of the house than that in which you usually practice. You still want to keep the area quiet and familiar but begin to teach the concept that your dog's name isn't just for certain rooms of the house. He needs to be listening for it in other settings, too.

Next, call your dog's name from a different room. This is tricky because your dog won't be able to see you. But by now, he knows his name and what it means, and you should hear those feet hit the floor and patter in your direction.

At this point, if you want to actually add a come command, you can. The word "here" or the actual word "come" are good choices. But always say your dog's name first, as in "Banner, here" or "Tassie, come!" Make sure both the name and the command are spoken in a clear and happy voice.

Now you can allow some minor distractions. You can have another, neutral person in the same room when you call, or a favorite toy left on the floor nearby. Or step outside and wander around the yard, and when your dog is checking on something else, call.

Snap on a retractable leash and walk through parks or quiet streets, always being ready to call and treat, call and treat.

As distractions increase and your request gets harder for your dog to obey, your reward should get better when he does choose to listen. Offer two or three wonderful treats when he comes to you in these situations.

The recall is very similar to playing the trade game. But instead of giving up something fun to eat or play with, your dog is essentially giving up his freedom. Make it matter. Make yourself the best thing in his expanding plethora of options. Make yourself worth the trade.

Scope out a place and let your dog loose in an unfamiliar, fenced area. Carry lots of those awesome treats with you, wait until he's had a minute or so to explore and get curious, then call. When he comes, give those goodies and a lot of them. Release and repeat. Over and over. Do this in as many new and safe locations as you can find.

If your dog doesn't respond to your first command, give the leash a tug, let him see that handful of treats, and then call again. If he's already off leash in a fenced area, call again with more energy, and run backward with your bag of treats when he looks at you. When he comes, treat, put the leash on again, and train with it on for a few more minutes.

This is a process. Don't rush it, and don't be afraid or embarrassed to take a few steps back in your training and once again work on the basics.

Above all else, force yourself to remember that your dog should never be punished for coming to you when you call. I don't know how many times I've seen it happen that a dog will be getting into trouble, the owner will call, and the dog will return as requested, only to be scolded and yelled at. This does not work. The dog may have been doing something naughty, but the dog coming on command is the important thing, and if that behavior is punished, you can guess how the dog will learn to feel about the recall in future.

If your dog comes to you, you owe him a reward. If he was being a brat beforehand, there are other commands you can give before he returns, such as "leave it" which might offer a little more correction. But that recall should never be compromised.

In a scenario where your dog has gotten away with something and then comes back to you, praise your dog for coming, then take him to the problem area on leash and discipline as you need to. You want your dog to associate the correction with the bad thing, not with returning to you and choosing to leave it alone.

Don't allow your dog to fail on the recall. If you're thrown into a surprise situation where your dog gets loose and you know he will not come back to you, then don't give a recall command. It will only teach your dog that he can actually blow you off and have more fun without you. Some tricks you can try if your dog does get away from you are to run the other direction while making happy sounds; sitting or lying down on the ground; ignoring your dog and giving lavish attention to another dog; or throwing and squeaking a favorite toy. It all depends on the specific situation and, of course, on the specific dog. Many people have excellent success by getting in the car and inviting their loose, car-loving dog to hop in for a joy ride around the block.

The bottom line is that you should never call your dog to come if you know that he won't.

If you think that he might, and if you have your treats handy, then feel free to try. Be sure to make a big scene, shaking your bag of goodies, crouching down to be at your dog's level, and moving backward slightly to encourage him to gravitate to you. Once you have him safely on a leash again, be generous with those cookies.

However, if one or two upbeat, encouraging calls don't bring your dog running, don't keep repeating the come command. If your dog hasn't returned within the first minute or less, chances are he's not going to. Your continued calling will only get you frustrated, and worse still, it will rapidly condition your dog not to respond correctly.

Another critical step in the recall is to catch your dog by the collar. Make sure he knows this is okay, and that it's part of the package. Accustom your dog to having your hand tucked into his collar. Teach him to follow when you gently tug him by the collar, not just by the leash. Be sure he understands that this is a normal part of the recall and is not a confusing or threatening gesture. When there's a loose dog who needs to be caught, be double sure you grab that collar before you begin pouring on the treats. Just like the trade game, make sure the dog can't grab back his freedom before you've grabbed his collar.

Take your time teaching the recall. Don't ask for too much too fast. Be realistic and careful. And keep the recall positive and fantastic. This is an exercise you will need to work on throughout your dog's entire life. Stick with it.

The trick to training a reliable recall is to make yourself super special to your dog by providing incredible treats and sincere praise. It's absolutely necessary, because of just how special your dog already is to you.

Tip 19

Do Something Together

You and your dog are friends. You do life together. If you do it right, that means long walks, random road trips, and lots of snuggle time.

You give to each other, and you get each other. And that is as it should be.

However, hanging out in the house and kicking back on the couch can only take you so far. Even pounding the pavement and walking together for an hour a day won't take you that extra mile.

There is so much more to a relationship with a dog. Friendship is great. But partnership can be even better.

Find something that you and your best friend can work at together. The powerful connection of a working relationship is a bond that cannot be attained in any other way short of literally working for it. The dynamic of working together, learning together, and excelling together is special and unique. There's nothing else like it.

Working with your dog will give each of you a much deeper understanding of the other. It will solidify your relationship. It will give both of you purpose. It will enlarge your dog's love and respect for you, and it will do the same for your love and respect toward your dog. And, as the two of you begin to see progress, achieve goals, and even capture titles and ribbons, it will give both of you joy and even more fulfillment.

These days, there are almost unlimited options when it comes to canine sports and competitions. Some are breed specific, but most are not. Following are a few of the activities which are most popular and easy to find.

❧ Obedience

Competition obedience is much more than just sit, lie down, and stay. Dogs and handlers negotiate various exercises including jumps, retrieves, hand signals, heeling patterns, and scent discrimination. Obedience is precise, intense, and mentally stimulating to both dogs and handlers.

❧ Agility

A fun and fast-paced sport, agility is the quintessential obstacle course for dogs. Standard courses involve jumps, tunnels, weave poles, and several large, contact obstacles like the teeter-totter. Handlers pilot their dogs through the course in a specific sequence, and dogs are judged on both speed and accuracy.

❧ Rally

This is an offshoot of obedience, but it's a little less formal and less intimidating for newcomers. Dog and handler teams navigate through a specified course of numbered stations, each of which requires them to perform a certain exercise. Rally is largely based on heel work, and also incorporates jumps. It's a great way to get both you and your dog started in ring competition.

❧ Tracking

As the name implies, dogs who participate in tracking are taught to follow a trail of human scent. Depending on the level of competition, tracks can include turns, different surfaces, cross-tracks, and dropped items for the dog to locate.

❧ Scent Work

Again, this sport encourages dogs to use their phenomenal sense of smell. Scent work requires dogs to identify several unique odors and to indicate their presence in various environments, such as indoors, outdoors, inside a vehicle, or underground.

❧ Tricks

Anything and everything from super simple to highly complex, and from useful to cute. At the more advanced levels, the handler combines multiple tricks into a scripted story, which is then acted out by the dog.

❧ Barn Hunt

This sport attempts to re-create the original purpose of many farm dogs as vermin catchers. Barn hunt competitions take place in an arena stacked with hay bales throughout which caged rats are hidden. Dogs must find and indicate however many rats have been concealed in the piles and tunnels of hay.

❧ Lure Coursing

Once open only to fast-running sight hounds, this sport now has classes open to any breed. Coursing allows a dog to chase a mechanical lure at top speed, and points are also awarded for focus and accuracy.

❧ Disc Dogs

All you need for this activity is a handful of Frisbees, an open field, and a dog who loves to fetch. Disc dog routines can be as basic or elaborate as you and your dog want them to be, incorporating everything from high-flying catches to vaults off the handler's back.

❧ Dock Diving

Perfect for dogs who love to swim and retrieve. Enticed by a toy, canine participants are trained to jump from a high ramp into a deep tank of water. Points are awarded based on components of the jump, including its height and distance.

❧ Canine Freestyle

A/k/a: Dancing with your dog. Freestyle is essentially heelwork choreographed to music. Far beyond basic walking, it utilizes spins, leg-weaves, pivots, props and more, synchronized to the rhythm of a favorite song.

These canine sports are only some of the possibilities open to you and your working dog. There are many other options. Some of them are breed specific, such as herding trials, field trials, and earth-dog events. Others are open to all breeds and mixed breeds.

Mostly, your decision as to which sport you get involved with comes down to your dog's natural talents and abilities. Do what your dog likes to do, and you'll find that you enjoy doing it yourself.

If you're the kind of person who not only loves working with dogs but who also likes working with people, there are opportunities for you as well.

Therapy dogs are trained and evaluated to go into a variety of facilities and interact with patients and residents. Nursing homes, hospitals, hospice care, and certain school settings are only some examples. People in distress, or those with special needs, often respond better to dogs than they do to other people. Certified therapy canines are allowed to pay regular visits to these facilities so that residents can pet them, hug them, and talk to them.

If you have a steady, affectionate dog who loves folks, and if you feel that you yourself possess the time and emotional strength that will be required, then therapy training might be right for both of you.

Some schools also welcome dogs as reading buddies for children who struggle with literacy. Dogs are quiet and nonjudgmental, and some students find it much easier to practice reading to a dog rather than to a class or a teacher.

Canine search and rescue may also allow you and your high-energy pup to give back. Search dogs are hyper, driven, and athletic, and they and their human handlers are rigorously trained to locate people who are lost or trapped. This entails long searches over large areas of wilderness or piles of rubble. Search and rescue will take a lot of time and commitment on your part. But the reward for you, for your dog, and for the people you help will be immeasurable.

No matter what you and your dog decide to do together, you will both be the better for it. You'll both enjoy physical and mental exercise, and your hearts will become deeper and softer toward one another. You really will become best friends. Not just buddies, but true, working partners.

So get up, get out, and make something of yourselves. It is so worth it, and your dog will love you for it.

Tip 20
Let Your Dog Make You a Better Person

When I was a teenager, I was painfully shy. I could hardly talk to people. School was an endless nightmare. I was never part of a group, and if I ever was accidentally included, I never participated. Tears came easily. Conversation did not.

It goes without saying that I had basically zero friends.

The exception, of course, was my dogs. They were there for me. They strengthened me and supported me. They made me laugh, and they made me hope. They loved me.

When the incredible vista of dog training was flung wide open to me at about age twenty, they also began to accomplish something more in my life. In a very real sense, my dogs have made me who I am today.

Today I can talk to people, initiate and continue conversations, and lead group discussions. I can even get up in front of people, on both virtual and literal stages, and present myself and my story. I've been in the newspaper, on the radio, and on TV. I have a website and a Youtube channel. It still isn't easy, and it still calls for courage.

But I can do it. My dogs have made that possible.

I loved working with them so much that I began to interact with people.

I discovered that, if competition training was really on my bucket list, then I needed to come out of my shell. I needed to ask questions, answer questions, go places, act confident, and train out in public.

My dogs and I began attending classes and fun matches. Then we went to shows, and we began to earn titles. And eventually, I figured out the truth. I realized that, as much work and time and effort as I may have poured into them, they had done that and then some for me. They had, in fact, given me far more socialization than I had ever given them.

Let your dog do the same for you. This entire book thus far—a total of nineteen out of twenty things that you should do to raise a dog right—have all been centered on your own hard work and perseverance. And that's a good thing. It has been a constant theme throughout these chapters that owning a dog is a commitment which takes hard work and responsibility from you.

But living and working with a dog is not a one-way street. Dogs give even better than they get.

So let your dog make you a better person. Dogs will do that for you.

They're just good to be with. They will remind you of the simple goodness of daily life. And on a day that isn't so good, they'll offer comfort and constancy.

But yet again, it goes deeper than just the feel good factor. Dogs will make you work, too. They will pinpoint your weaknesses, and they'll help you overcome them if you allow it. Among many other things, your dog can teach you compassion, kindness, confidence, forgiveness, and throw a healthy dose of patience into the bargain. Maybe you'll overcome your own shyness. Maybe you'll learn to keep your anger in check. Maybe your dog will give you the boost you need to get out of the house, to get out of yourself, or even to get out of bed.

They come to us for so many reasons. Be open and honest about what those reasons might be for you.

Permit your dog to bring you back to basic joys. Let your dog challenge you to think, to learn, and to be creative. Allow this, your best friend, to challenge you to love.

It's necessary to stoke up your positive side around a dog, especially if you're training or traveling together. Carry that positivity into the rest of your day, the rest of your interactions, and the rest of your life. Let your dog teach you to hope.

No dog is perfect, but no person is, either. We really do make a great combination. Dogs and people were made for each other. We were made to be best friends. Catch that reality and keep it on a tight leash. And understand that, in the end, our dogs have so much more to teach us than we can ever teach to them.

Dog Treat
RECIPES

Salmon Brownies

2 14.75 ounces can salmon, undrained

1 egg

1/2 cup vegetable oil

4 cups flour

Combine first three ingredients in large bowl. Add flour, and enough water to form the consistency of cake or brownie batter. Mix well. Place in 9-by-13-inch pan. Bake at 350 degrees for about 35 minutes. Cool and cut into brownies. Store in the refrigerator, or freeze.

Banana Bones

4 cups whole wheat flour

2 cups Grape Nuts cereal

2 cups mashed banana (about 5 bananas total)

3/4 cup water

2 tbsp vegetable oil

2 tbsp honey

Mix thoroughly in large bowl. Roll out dough on floured surface to about 1/4-inch thickness. Cut into desired shapes. Bake at 325 degrees for 30-35 minutes. These cookies do last longer if stored in the fridge.

Tuna Fudge

2 6-ounce cans tuna (do not drain)

1-1/2 cups whole wheat flour

2 eggs, lightly beaten

1/4 cup Parmesan cheese

Combine all ingredients. Place in 9-by-9-inch pan and bake at 350 degrees for 20 minutes. Cool and cut into cubes. Store in the refrigerator, or freeze.

Peanut Butter Bones

4 cups whole wheat flour

2 cups wheat germ

2 cups peanut butter

1-1/2 cup water

1/4 cup honey

Mix thoroughly in large bowl. Roll out dough on floured surface to about 1/4-inch thickness. Cut into desired shapes. Bake at 325 degrees for 30-35 minutes. If you want harder cookies, leave in the oven for several hours after turning it off.

Carob Brownies

Carob is a great substitute for chocolate, which dogs love but absolutely cannot have!

1 cup brown rice flour

3/4 cup quick-cooking rolled oats

3 tsp carob powder

1/2 cup creamy peanut butter

2 large eggs

About 1 cup cold water

Combine all ingredients, except water. Then, beat in enough water to form a soft (but not a wet) batter. Press into an 8-inch baking pan. Bake at 350 degrees for about 15 minutes, until firm to the touch. Cool and cut into brownies.

Carob Cookies

1 cup peanut butter

2 eggs, slightly beaten

1 cup milk

2 cups whole wheat flour

2 tbsp sugar

1 tbsp baking powder

1 cup carob chips

Beat eggs with peanut butter, then add milk and combine well. In separate bowl combine flour, sugar, and baking powder. Add the dry mixture to the peanut butter mixture and mix well. Stir in carob chips. Drop by rounded teaspoons onto cookie sheet, leaving about one inch of space between cookies. Bake at 350 degrees for 20-25 minutes, until cookies are just barely dry in the middle.

Bowser's Birthday Cake

1 pound ground turkey or chicken

2 carrots, diced

1 10-ounce package frozen spinach, thawed and squeezed dry

1 cup cooked brown rice

1 tbsp vegetable oil

1 egg, slightly beaten

Combine all ingredients in large bowl and mix well. Pat mixture into greased and waxed paper-lined 9-inch cake pan. Bake at 350 degrees for 45-50 minutes. Keep refrigerated.

About the Author

Blind since the age of fifteen months, Reyna Bradford homesteads her own hobby farm in northeast Kansas. She has always loved animals, and currently shares her home with nine dogs, multiple cats, and Angora rabbits. She raises registered Nubian dairy goats and has learned to do all kinds of things with the milk, including making cheese, soap, and yogurt.

Reyna is passionate about training and showing her dogs in companion and performance events with the American Kennel Club. She is a proud Kansan who loves to share the beauty of her home state with her readers.

Besides her farm and her furkids, she also loves film scores, thunderstorms, and dark chocolate.

www.reynawrites.com
YouTube Channel: Sunshine & Reyna
Facebook: In My Hands – author Reyna Bradford

Stay up to date with what's happening on the farm, subscribe to Reyna's blog: reynawrites.com/blog

Made in the USA
Columbia, SC
18 February 2023